W9-DGX-253

SCIENCE ANSWERS

Electricity

FROM AMPS TO VOLTS

Heinemann Library
Chicago, Illinois

Christopher Cooper

Design: Jo Hinton-Malivoire and
   Tinstar Design Ltd (www.tinstar.co.uk)
Illustrations: Jeff Edwards
Picture Research: Rosie Garai
   and Lizz Eddison
Originated by Dot Gradations Ltd.
Printed in China by Wing King Tong

08 07 06 05 04
10 9 8 7 6 5 4 3 2 1

**Library of Congress Cataloging-in-
Publication Data**
Cooper, Christopher (Christopher Robin),
1944-
   Electricity : from amps to volts /
Christopher Cooper.
      v. cm. -- (Science answers)
Includes bibliographical references and
index.
Contents: What is electricity -- What is
electricity made of? -- What happens when
you turn on an electric switch? -- How does
electricity make things move? -- What are
amps, ohms, and volts? -- How does a
generator produce electricity? -- How do
batteries work? -- How is electricity used?
   ISBN 1-4034-0950-1 (HC), 1-4034-3547-2
(pbk.)
   1. Electricity--Juvenile literature. [1.
Electricity.] I. Title. II.
Series.
   QC527.2.C663 2003
   537--dc21
                    2003002502

Acknowledgments
The author and publishers are grateful to
the following for permission to reproduce
copyright material:

p. 4 Digital Stock; p.5 Jose Luis
Pelaez/Corbis; pp. 7, 25 Robert Harding;
p. 8 Tudor Photography; p.9 Roger
Harris/Science Photo Library; pp. 10, 12, 13,
19 Liz Eddison; p. 15 Photodisc; p. 17
Novosti Press Agency /Science Photo
Library; p. 22 Cordelia Molloy/Science
Photo Library; p. 23 Joseph Sohm/Corbis;
p. 26 A. Sternberg//Ferranti
Electronics/Science Photo Library; p. 28
Historical Picture Archive/Corbis.

Cover photograph reproduced with
permission of Richard Cummins/Corbis.

Every effort has been made to contact
copyright holders of any material
reproduced in this book. Any omissions will
be rectified in subsequent printings if notice
is given to the publishers.

Some words are shown in bold,
like this. You can find out
what they mean by looking in
the glossary

Contents

About the experiments and demonstrations

In this book you will find sections called Science Answers. They describe an activity that you can try yourself. Here are some safety rules to follow:

- Ask an adult to help with any cutting using a sharp knife.
- Never connect the two terminals of a **battery** directly together. The large **current** could burn you.
- Never connect a number of batteries to each other and then connect the last one directly to the first. The large current could burn you.
- Electrical sockets are dangerous. Never, ever try to experiment with them.
- Do not experiment with a car battery. It can deliver a dangerous shock.

Materials you will use

Most of these activities can be done with objects you can find in your own home. A few will need items you can buy from a hardware store. You will also need paper and a pencil to record your results.

What Is Electricity?

Your world depends on electricity. Electricity runs many of the things you use every day. Machines in your home are run by electricity—refrigerators, music systems, food blenders, room heaters, and power tools. Machines in offices also use electricity, including elevators, air conditioners, photocopiers, and many others. In factories, machines run by electricity melt metals and lift heavy objects. Other electrical machines drill, stamp, and shape materials. At home or at work people are constantly using lights, telephones, computers, radios, and TVs. All are run by electricity.

What is an electric current?

The electricity that makes a lightbulb glow or a fan turn is called an electric **current,** because it consists of moving electricity (just as a current of water consists of moving water). There are electric currents in nature, too. A stroke of lightning is a powerful but short-lived electric current.

Making light

Cities blaze with light at night, thanks to electricity. Artificial lighting used to be produced by burning oil or candles. Little work was done after sunset and people went to bed early. When electric lighting became widespread, people continued their daytime activities into the night. Today the centers of large cities are busy 24 hours a day.

How do machines use electricity?

Even when electricity does not provide the actual power that runs a machine, it often helps to make it work. A car engine runs on gasoline, but electricity is needed to start the engine. Then, while the engine is running, electricity makes the sparks that make the gasoline burn. Electrical instruments send information to the driver about how the engine is working. Many of the driver's controls, such as the indicators and the horn, use electricity.

Pocket power

Mobile phones also need electricity. At the heart of a mobile phone are microchips as complex as those in personal computers. They work by small electric currents provided by **batteries,** which are **portable** stores of electricity.

What Is Electricity Made Of?

An electric **current** is made up of a stream of **particles.** Different kinds of particles can make electric currents. But the most common electric current is made up of a particular kind of particle called an **electron.** Electrons are parts of **atoms.** All the matter around you is made up of atoms. They are so small that a line of a hundred million atoms would stretch across your fingernail.

Electrons make up the outer layers of each atom and move around a tiny central part called the nucleus (plural *nuclei*) of the atom. The electrons have an electric **charge,** which is the scientific name for "amount of electricity." The nucleus consists of a different sort of particle called a **proton.**

How does an electric current flow?

Many sorts of atoms can lose electrons easily. Metals are an example. In a metal wire the electrons can easily be forced to separate from the atoms and flow through the wire. This stream of electrons is an electric current.

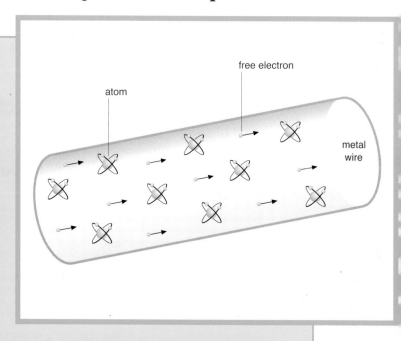

There are wires in **devices** such as radios and TVs, and cables (which are just thick wires) carry electricity to homes. They are made of metal—often copper—so that the electrons can move easily.

Is there just one kind of electric charge?

Electrons and protons have different kinds of electric charges. An electron has a negative charge. Protons have a positive charge. If an object gains electrons, the object has a negative charge. If it loses electrons, it has a positive charge, because it then has more protons than electrons in its atoms. Friction is one way that objects can gain or lose electrons. Positive and negative charges attract each other, but all negative charges repel each other, or push each other away. All positive charges also repel each other. A short way of saying this is, "like charges repel, unlike charges attract."

Lightning strike

Lightning is electricity in movement. A stream of electrons flows for a fraction of a second from a storm cloud to the ground, or from one cloud to another cloud. The air along the path of the current is heated to about 50,000 °F (about 30,000 °C). This hot air glows and you see the path of the electric current as a bright, zigzagging line—the lightning flash.

EXPERIMENT: How can you give something an electric charge?

HYPOTHESIS

Some materials lose or gain **electrons** when they are rubbed together. This causes an electric **charge.**

EQUIPMENT

Balloon and clothing (for example, a sweater)

EXPERIMENT STEPS

1. Rub the balloon against a piece of clothing, such as a sweater. It will probably stick to the clothing.
2. If this works, put the balloon next to your hair. The balloon attracts your hair too, making the individual strands stand up when the balloon is held near it.
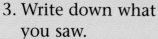
3. Write down what you saw.

CONCLUSION

The rubbing moves some electrons between the balloon and the sweater. The balloon and sweater each began with exactly equal amounts of positive and negative charges. After rubbing, one has slightly less negative charge and the other has slightly more. These charges are called **static electricity** (*static* means that the charges are at rest). The balloon and

the sweater therefore attract each other. The experiment cannot tell you which way the electrons moved. In fact, electrons tend to move from materials such as wool, cotton, or nylon to latex. In this experiment, the electrons almost certainly moved from the clothing to the balloon.

How can you use static electricity?

A photocopying machine uses static electricity. A light in the machine shines an **image** of a page of a book, for example, onto a heated rotating drum. The drum has a positive electric charge on its surface. The light knocks electrons out of **atoms** under the surface of the drum, and these cancel out some of the positive charge. Where the original page is lighter, more light shines through and more electrons are produced. So there is less positive charge on the drum in these parts of the image.

The drum's electrical charge attracts a black powder called toner. There is more toner where there is more charge. When the drum rolls over blank paper, it presses toner onto the paper and melts it to form a permanent image.

When do we "see" electricity?

Electrons and nuclei in all things—even your own body—push and pull each other all the time. But the total amount of positive charge in any piece of matter is normally exactly equal to the total amount of negative charge. This is because normally there are exactly as many **protons** as electrons in each atom. (You can see the electrons [blue] and protons [red] in this computer-generated artwork of an atom.) So the total electrical **force** between two objects is normally zero. To create electric effects, positive and negative charges somehow need to be separated from each other.

What Happens When You Turn on an Electric Switch?

The electric **current** used in homes and workplaces travels along cables from giant **power** stations. When the current arrives, you need to be able to control it to make it work for you. A switch is one way of doing this. When you flip an electric light switch, you start a current flowing through the bulb. You stop the current by flipping the switch off.

How does the switch work?

The electric current travels along metal wires from the power station. It is easy for a current to move through metals. When the switch is on, the current can continue along wires into the lamp, radio, or other **device.** When you turn the switch off, the switch makes a gap that the current cannot cross. When you turn the switch on again, you close the gap so that the current can flow into the device once more.

Contact!

If you take apart an old flashlight that isn't needed any more, you may be able to see how the switch works. Turning it on brings two pieces of metal together to make a path for the current. Turning it off pulls the pieces of metal apart. This leaves a gap that the current cannot cross.

What materials can a current flow through easily?

The wires used in electrical devices are made of metal. Metal has very low **resistance,** which means a current can move through it easily. Low-resistance materials and things made from them are called **conductors.** Wood, rubber, and most plastics are examples of **insulators,** which block currents. Electrical wires have plastic covers to keep currents from leaking out. Engineers working on an electrical **apparatus** wear plastic-soled shoes to prevent currents from passing through their bodies to the ground. Electricity can only flow if the **circuit** is complete. Because plastic does not conduct electricity, the plastic soles cause a break in the circuit.

How does a control knob work?

The volume control knob on a radio is an example of another type of control. Turning the knob changes the length of wire that the current flows through. The current is made weaker by having to flow through a longer wire. Scientists and engineers say that the longer wire has a greater resistance, because it stops the current from moving so easily.

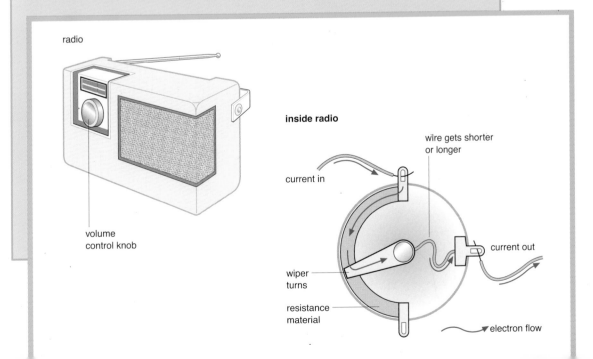

radio

volume
control knob

inside radio

current in

wire gets shorter
or longer

current out

wiper
turns

resistance
material

electron flow

11

Turn it up!

An electric current works the loudspeaker in a radio. The stronger the current, the louder the sound. The current flows into a coil of wire on its way to the loudspeaker. When the volume control is turned down, the current is made to go along the whole coil. The **resistance** of the coil is high, and this makes the current weak. When the control is turned up, the current goes along only a small part of the coil. This small part of the coil has a small resistance, and so the current is stronger.

How Does Electricity Make Things Move?

Electric **charges** cause two sorts of **force.** When the charges are **stationary** they cause electrostatic forces (*static* means "at rest"). After you have rubbed a balloon against your clothes, the balloon and the clothes have stationary charges or **static electricity** on them. The force of attraction between them is electrostatic. The second kind of force is caused by a moving charge— an electric **current.** This force is magnetic. A magnetic force is the type of force that affects a compass needle. For example, when there is lightning nearby, a compass needle twitches. It is pulled by the magnetic forces from the powerful current of the lightning rod. Forces caused by electric currents are called electromagnetic.

What is electromagnetism?

The effects of electromagnetism are all around you. A compass needle points north–south because of the earth's magnetism. This magnetism is caused by electric currents in the earth's core, which consists of hot, molten iron. Every machine or **appliance** that contains an **electric motor,** such as a coffee grinder or a vacuum cleaner, uses electromagnetism generated by an **electromagnet,** similar to the one shown here. The electric current going into the **device** is used to generate a force, which turns the moving parts.

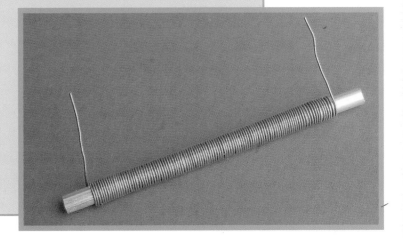

EXPERIMENT: How does electricity make things move?

HYPOTHESIS
Electric **charges** can attract or repel other objects, causing them to move.

EQUIPMENT
Paper, plastic comb, sink with a tap or burette, as shown in the picture

EXPERIMENT STEPS
1. Tear the paper into small pieces.
2. Run a plastic (not metal) comb through your hair several times quickly.
3. Hold the comb close to the pieces of paper. You'll see the pieces jump up and stick to the comb. If they do not, try a comb made of another kind of plastic.
4. Now run water from a tap. Have the tap only slightly open, so that the water is a slow, thin stream. Run the comb through your hair again and hold it near the top of the stream of water.
5. Write down what you saw.

CONCLUSION
After you combed you hair, there were **electrons** on the plastic that were removed from your hair. They attracted the water and the paper in the same way that a balloon rubbed against clothes attracts the clothes. This is an electrostatic **force.**

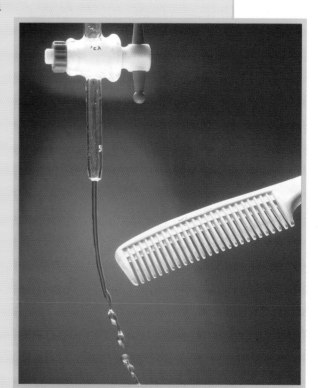

What Are Amps, Ohms, and Volts?

Scientists measure the amount of electricity in units called **coulombs** (symbol C). One coulomb is the amount of charge of about 6 quintillion electrons.

Electric **currents** are described in amps (symbol A). A current of 1 amp is 1 coulomb of charge flowing every second. An electric current needs a push to make it flow. The amount of push is measured in volts (symbol V) and is called **voltage.** How much current flows depends on the voltage pushing it and the **resistance** of the **circuit** that it flows through. The unit of resistance is the ohm (symbol Ω, a Greek letter pronounced "omega").

Just about the size of it

Here are some facts about typical household electric **appliances:**

Current used
Typical electric coffeepot: 4 amps
Typical lightbulb: 0.4 amp
Pocket calculator: 0.07 amp

Voltage
AA-size **batteries:** 1.5 volts
Electrical outlets: in many countries, about 110 volts

Resistance
Typical electric coffeepot: about 25 ohms
Typical lightbulb: about 600 ohms

The right voltage for the job

An electric current is carried from electricity generating stations across the country along metal wires slung from towers called **pylons.** This current is at several hundred thousand volts, because this is best for sending currents long distances.

It would be dangerous to use very high voltages in factories, offices, or homes. So the cross-country cables lead to **substations,** where machines called **transformers** automatically reduce the voltage. Some cables then take electricity to factories, while others take a still lower-voltage supply to homes.

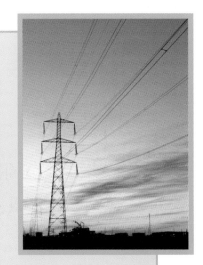

How Does a Generator Produce Electricity?

An electric **current** produces its own magnetism, but the reverse also happens. If magnetism passes through an electric **circuit** and the magnetism varies in strength or direction, a **voltage** is produced in the circuit. If the magnetism does not change, but the circuit moves, a voltage is also produced in the circuit.

What happens in a **power** station **generator** is more complicated. The **stationary** part of the generator is an **electromagnet,** and its **magnetic field** passes through the coils of the **rotor.** When the coils spin, a voltage is produced in the rotor. The spinning motion generates electricity at about 25,000 volts.

In a very simple generator, an electric current can be produced just by rotating a coil of wire between the poles, or ends, of a magnet.

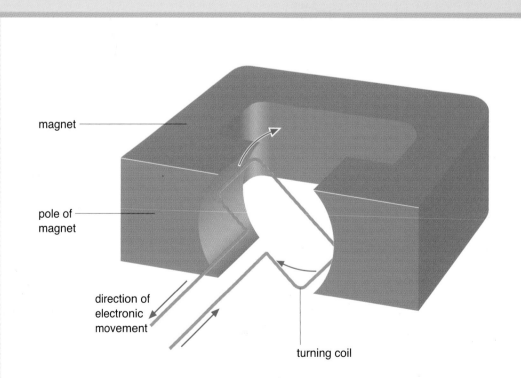

magnet

pole of magnet

direction of electronic movement

turning coil

Electricity for homes, offices, and factories is produced by generators in power stations. In most power stations the rotor is turned by steam. The steam is produced when water is heated by burning fossil fuels such as oil, gas, and coal. Nuclear **energy** can also be used. Hydroelectric power stations use the power of falling water. Electricity can also be generated by solar panels, which change the energy of sunlight into electricity.

Two-way current

The current produced by a spinning generator in a power station is not a one-way current. It goes in one direction, then in the other. It is called an **alternating current (AC).** (*Alternating* means "reversing.") Many machines, such as drills and some **appliances** work better on an AC than **direct current (DC). Transformers** also need AC to work with.

Wet electricity

One way to run electricity generators uses **hydroelectric energy.** This is the power provided by steep waterfalls on rivers or water flowing out of reservoirs (artificial lakes made by dams). This form of electricity generation works well in mountainous areas.

What are other ways to generate electricity?

Electricity can be generated by wind **power.** A wind turbine is a giant fan turned by the wind. Wind farms, made up of dozens or hundreds of wind turbines, have been built in a few windy places. A very large wind farm can produce as much electricity as an ordinary power station.

Ocean waves also have been used to generate electricity. One type of wave-power **device** is a duck. It is a floating hollow canister fastened to the seabed. About 25 ducks are linked together in a chain. They rock as waves pass, and the turning motion is used to turn an electricity **generator.** The electricity is sent to the shore along a cable. Hundreds of chains of ducks working together can produce a useful amount of electricity.

Solar energy

Another source of **energy** for electricity generation is the energy of sunlight, or solar energy. Very large **installations** have been built in which hundreds of large mirrors reflect sunlight onto a boiler, raising its temperature enough to boil the water. The steam then drives a generator in the usual way.

Photoelectric cells

More commonly, smaller power units are used in which **photoelectric cells** generate electricity directly from the energy of sunlight. When sunlight falls on photoelectric cells, they produce a weak **voltage.** Solar energy is used to generate electricity in pocket calculators, on spacecraft, and in remote scientific research stations.

Scientists' fears

Some scientists argue that people should reduce the amount of gas, oil, coal, and uranium that they use. They think oil will run out soon and the carbon dioxide produced by burning oil and coal will cause the atmosphere to trap more of the sun's energy.

This is called global warming. It would raise the temperature of the earth. There are also fears that nuclear energy produces dangerous and long-lasting radioactive waste.

 • SCIENCE ANSWERS •

DEMONSTRATION: Light on the problem

If you have a solar-powered calculator, you can see the effect of altering the amount of light that falls on it.

DEMONSTRATION STEPS

1. Turn the calculator on. See what happens to the display if you shade the photoelectric cells. (These are visible as a dark panel on the top of the calculator.)

2. See what happens when you shine a bright light onto the cells, but do not make the calculator or the photoelectric cells hot by bringing a lamp too close.

3. Write down what you saw.

CONCLUSION

The photoelectric cells stop working when light stops shining on them, or soon after. They work better when the light is brighter.

How Do Batteries Work?

Batteries are handy and **portable** stores of electricity. Chemical reactions inside them generate electricity. Each battery has two terminals, or metal contacts. In some types of batteries, there are two studs at the top. In others, two metal strips stick out at the top. In small button batteries used in watches and calculators, the top and bottom of the metal case are the two contacts.

When an external **circuit** is connected to the battery's terminals, the chemical reactions begin. These reactions cause **electrons** to flow from one terminal to the other inside the battery. The stream of electrons then continues out of the battery. The electrons flow along **conductors,** such as copper wires, through a **device** such as a lamp or a radio. They then flow back into the battery.

What are batteries called?

The correct name for most of the batteries you use is *cell*. The word *battery* should be strictly applied to only several cells joined together. A 1.5-volt battery is actually a cell. A 9-volt battery consists of six 1.5-volt cells joined together. A car battery typically consists of six 2-volt cells.

How are batteries constructed?

Every cell has two **electrodes** made of different materials. In one type of AA battery, one electrode is the zinc case of the cell. The other electrode is a carbon rod inside, connected to a metal cap on the cell. In every cell there is a special material between the two electrodes, called the electrolyte. In a flashlight battery this material is a paste that contains chemicals. In a car battery it is a liquid, dilute sulphuric acid.

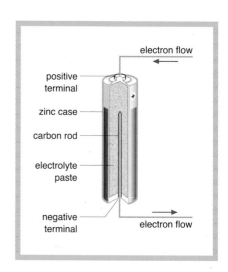

electron flow

positive terminal

zinc case

carbon rod

electrolyte paste

negative terminal

electron flow

EXPERIMENT: Can you make a simple battery?

HYPOTHESIS
You can make a battery by dipping two different metals into acid. Follow the steps below to find out how this works.

EQUIPMENT
Four small pieces of copper, 4 small pieces of zinc, 4 potatoes, 5 pieces of electrical wire, 8 alligator clips, flashlight bulb in a bulb holder. If you cannot find strips of metal, use large screws or nails of different metals.

EXPERIMENT STEPS

1. Stick a piece of zinc and copper into a potato and attach the wires as shown.
2. Touch the other ends of the wires to your tongue. The tingle and strange taste are caused by a weak electric **current** from your battery!
3. Now connect the four potatoes as shown in the diagram. You should be able to get enough **voltage** from them to make the lightbulb glow.
4. Write down what you saw.

CONCLUSION
Dipping two different metals into acid can make a battery. Potatoes have enough acid inside them to make a battery.

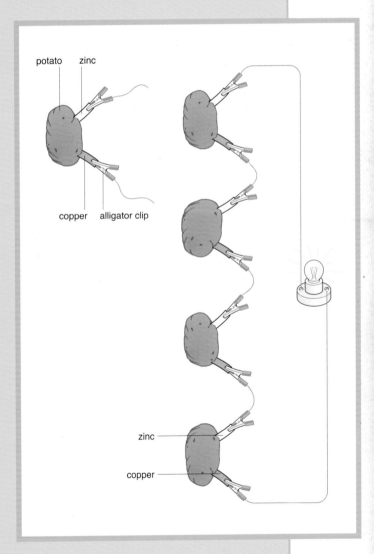

potato   zinc

copper   alligator clip

zinc

copper

How Is Electricity Used?

One way in which electricity is useful is in making heat and light. An electric lightbulb contains a wire made of a metal such as tungsten. The wire is heated by the **current** passing through it and glows white-hot.

The wire gets hot because the **electrons** moving in the current bump against the **atoms** of the metal, making the atoms vibrate faster. Heat *is* the vibration of atoms.

The more the electrons bump against the atoms, the harder it is for the current to flow—that is, the higher the **resistance** of the wire. So a high-resistance wire produces more heat.

Warmth from electricity

Electrical heat can also be used for itself, not just as a means of making light. In an oven, the current heats coils of wire built into the hot plates. Heat passes from the coils into the hot plates.

The same idea is used in space heaters, irons, and electric frying pans. In a hair dryer, coils of wire are heated. The same current drives a fan, which blows a stream of air over the hot coils.

Can electricity make movement?

An **electric motor** is like an electric **generator** in reverse. In the generator, rotation causes an electric current to flow. In the motor, the electric current causes rotation. The motor contains a **rotor,** which consists of a set of coils that act as **electromagnets** when a current flows. Surrounding the rotor is either a set of magnets or an armature, which consists of coils of wire that also act as electromagnets when a current flows. The magnetic **forces** make the rotor turn.

Motors like this turn household fans and hair dryers. In a car an electric motor is used to start the gasoline engine. Smaller electric motors open and close windows in some cars. Many trains are driven by electric motors. The electricity may be supplied from a **power** rail or overhead power lines. Or it may be produced by a diesel engine in the locomotive. Some cars also use electric motors. They need to recharge their **batteries** at refueling stations such as the one shown here.

How is sound turned into electricity?

Sound reproduction depends on the production of an electric **current** with a strength that is **variable** from moment to moment in the same way that the loudness of the sound is variable.

A very simple kind of microphone is used in telephones. The sound of the user's voice makes a metal plate in the telephone's microphone vibrate. The plate presses against tiny grains of carbon, alternately harder, reducing the **resistance,** and more gently, increasing the resistance. A small electric current constantly passes through the carbon. As the resistance changes, the current changes in strength.

How is electricity turned back into sound?

When the current from a telephone microphone is passed into a telephone loudspeaker, it goes through a coil, which acts like an **electromagnet.** The coil attracts a magnet attached to a cone-shaped piece of metal or other material. The rapidly changing current causes the strength of the magnetism to change rapidly. This in turn causes the cone to vibrate.

The vibrating cone sets up vibrations in the air. These vibrations are sounds, because a sound is simply a vibration in the air. The sounds are a copy of the sounds that struck the microphone.

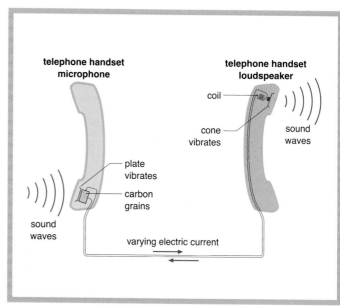

How does electricity make pictures?

The lens on the front of a TV camera forms an **image** inside the camera. The electronics inside the camera read this image from side to side and from top to bottom, many times per second.

Inside the TV receiver tube, beams of **electrons** sweep from side to side and top to bottom, painting the picture on the inside of the screen. The electrons strike dots of materials that then glow. The stronger the beam (that is, the more electrons in it), the brighter the material glows.

What are microchips?

At the heart of almost every electronic **device** today is a microchip. This is a small piece of **semiconductor** material. Semiconductors allow a **current** to pass, but less easily than a **conductor** does. The elements silicon and germanium are examples. Semiconductors have special properties that make them valuable for building electrical **circuits.**

A microchip is usually about 0.16 square inches (6 square millimeters). On its surface is a circuit made by adding small quantities of other materials in the pattern of the circuit. The circuit can contain millions of electronic **components.**

How do computers use microchips?

Inside a personal computer, a small number of microchips work together. One is the CPU, or central processing unit. This is the "brain" of the computer. Other chips control the monitor display, the sound, and other functions. Each microchip is packaged in a plastic container, with metal pins sticking out. The pins make contact with the PCB, or printed circuit board. This is a board that carries a circuit of copper pathways, which are printed on a flat surface. Microchips and other components can be plugged in at various points around the board. There is even a fan to cool the inside of the computer.

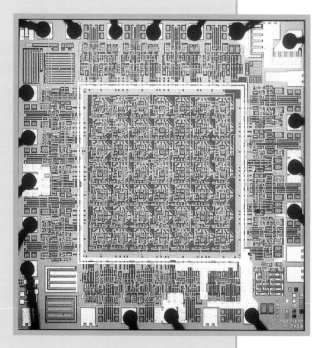

EXPERIMENT: How does the electricity supplied affect how a motor runs?

HYPOTHESIS
A motor can be driven by electricity. Other components connected in a series mean that less **power** reaches the motor.

EQUIPMENT
Small **electric motor,** 2 flat 4.5 V **batteries,** several lengths of wire, 1 bulb and bulb holder

EXPERIMENT STEPS
1. You may find an electric motor inside a battery-powered toy car or inside a hand-held fan. Ask an adult to help you remove it.
2. Test the motor using batteries and the setup shown in the diagram.
3. Touch the wires from the battery terminals to the motor's contacts and watch the motor turn.
4. Try putting extra **resistance** in the circuit—for example, a flashlight bulb.
5. Write down what you saw.

CONCLUSION
When components are connected in a series, each one receives less electricity. If another battery is added, the supply of electricity to the circuit increases.

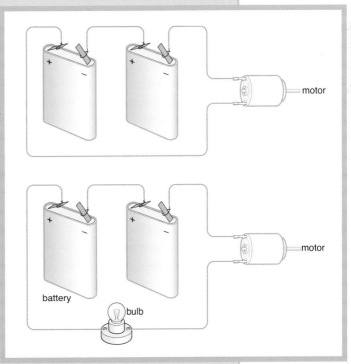

André Marie Ampère (1775–1836)

French scientist André Marie Ampère was one of the first scientists to make it clear that electricity and magnetism are closely connected. He discovered how the strength of an electric **current's magnetic field** is related to the strength of the current and the length of the **conductor** through which it flows. And he discovered how two wires carrying electric currents attract each other or push each other apart, depending on the direction of the currents.

Michael Faraday (1791–1867)

Michael Faraday studied how electric currents make chemical reactions happen. He also found that changing a magnetic field can make an electric current flow. This is the basis of modern electricity generation.

Faraday found it much easier to think in pictures than in mathematical symbols. He invented the way of showing magnetic fields as lines of **force** that is widely used today.

Amazing Facts

- Some fish use electricity as a weapon. The torpedo fish can grow up to 6 feet (1.8 meters) long and can repeatedly deliver an electric current into the surrounding water. Small fish nearby are stunned, and the torpedo fish can easily catch and eat them. The electric eel, which grows up to 10 feet (3 meters) long, can do the same. Some fish produce weaker electric currents, which they use to send signals to each other or to find obstacles in the water.

- The **battery** was invented by an Italian scientist who was so fascinated by electricity that he even wrote a poem about it in Latin. Alessandro Volta experimented with different metals to try to make an electric current. By 1800 he had succeeded. His first battery used curved bars of copper and zinc dipped into bowls of salty water. Later, Volta improved the design by stacking disks of copper, zinc, and cardboard soaked in salty water. A current would flow when the top and bottom of this pile were connected.

- It is often said that "lightning doesn't strike in the same place twice." This is actually wrong! The tallest tree or building in an area is likely to be struck whenever there's a thunderstorm. The tallest skyscrapers may be struck hundreds of times a year. Tall buildings are equipped with lightning conductors—strips of metal that run from the top of the building into the ground. The electricity of the lightning usually flows harmlessly along this.

- In the mid–18th century, Benjamin Franklin, scientist and one of the founders of the United States, entertained dinner guests with a turkey that he tried to kill with an electric shock. He cooked the meat before a fire lit by an electric spark. Franklin also gave his guests glasses previously **charged** with **static electricity.** He enjoyed their reactions as they received mild shocks.

Glossary

alternating current (AC) electricityt that flows first one way and then the other

apparatus equipment used for a particular purpose

appliance another word for device, often used when talking about machinery in the home

atom smallest piece of a chemical element that can exist on its own. It consists of smaller particles, including electrons and protons.

battery device that generates electric currents by a chemical reaction

charge amount of electricity. Charge can be of two kinds, called positive and negative.

circuit arrangement of electrical parts through which a current can flow to do a job

component part of something larger, usually a machine

conductor material or object that an electric current can flow through

coulomb unit of electric charge equal to the charge carried by 6.28 quintillion electrons

current flow of electric charge

device something made for a special purpose

direct current (DC) electric current that flows in one direction all the time

electric motor machine that converts electrical energy into motion

electrode conductor through which electrons enter and leave an electrical device

electromagnet device that develops a magnetic field when an electric current is passed through it

electron negatively charged particle found in every atom. Most electric currents are a flow of electrons and protons.

energy measure of a system's ability to make things happen: move objects, generate heat or light, make chemical reactions occur, and so on

force a push or a pull

generator machine for producing an electric current. It is usually driven by steam.

hydroelectric energy electrical energy generated by a river or a stream of water from a lake or reservoir

image picture of something

installation something that is placed somewhere for a particular purpose

insulator material or object that an electric current cannot easily flow through

magnetic field area around a magnet through which electric current flows

photoelectric cell device that generates electricity when light strikes it

particle tiny piece of matter

portable able to be carried around easily

power rate at which energy is transferred from one place to another; energy put to work, for example, nuclear power, electrical power, and steam power

proton positively charged particle found in every atom. Most electric currents are a flow of protons and electrons.

pylon tall mast that carries electricity cables

resistance measure of how easily an electric current passes through something

rotor rotating coil in an electric motor or generator

semiconductor material with a resistance between that of an insulator and a conductor. Microchips are made from semiconductors.

static electricity nonmoving electric charge on an object, due to its losing or gaining electrons

stationary not moving

substation place where the voltage of the electricity supply is reduced for use in factories, offices, and homes

transformer device for changing the voltage of an alternating current

variable not always the same; capable of changing

voltage push that makes an electric current flow. Voltage is produced by chemical reactions, magnetism, or other means.

▶• Index

▶• More Books to Read

Oxlade, Chris. *Science Topics: Electricity and Magnetism.* Chicago:
    Heinemann Library, 1999.

Parker, Steve. *Science Fact Files: Electricity and Magnetism.* Austin,
    Tex.: Raintree Publishers, 2000

Searle, Bobbi. *Electricity and Magnetism.* Brookfield, Conn.:
    Millbrook Press, Inc., 2002.